DROWNING

Copyright ©2021 Denoma Publishing LLC
All rights reserved. No part of this book may be reproduced or used in any manner without written permission of the copyright owner except for the use of quotations in a book review.

ISBN: 978-1-7371422-0-1

LCCN: 2021908631

PUBLISHER: Denoma Publishing LLC

Disclaimer

The information provided it in this book is design to provide helpful information on the subjects discussed. The book is not meant to be used, nor should it be used, to diagnose or treat any medical conditions. For any diagnosis or treatment of any medical problem you may be experiencing, consult your own physician. The publisher and author are not responsible for any specific health conditions (mental or physical) that may require medical supervision and are not liable for any damages or negative consequences of any treatment action application or preparation, to any person reading or following the information in this book. All the information obtained in this book is from the author's own personal experience and perspective.

Drowning
You **Can't Breathe** Water!
How I Survived

Charmion Sparrow

Denoma Publishing LLC

DEDICATION

I want to dedicate this book to my dear sister, Charlotte Breeden. She is no longer with me, and I grieve her loss still today. She would indeed be very proud of me for sharing my story. She also suffered from depression and would have been the one person that helped me through my battle had she been around. I cherish the moments we shared. I know she would have been my biggest fan. I love you dearly and miss you tremendously.

ACKNOWLEDMENT

I want to thank God for holding my hand, walking beside me, and loving me unconditionally. I thank Him for my peace as well as my struggles. I want to thank my mom, Betty Sparrow, for being so hard me, which molded me into the strong woman I am today. She taught me how to value myself and never accept mess from anyone. That is right. Mess. I thank my dad, Charles Sparrow, who is shining down from heaven, for teaching me to be the entrepreneur I am today. He taught me how to figure things out until you get it right. I want to thank my handsome son, Jamarcus James, who motivates me to be a great example to him. He has been the reason I keep my head up. He has been the reason I never quit. I want to also thank, Virginia Hayes, who was my Sunday School teacher, mentor, friend, and book editor. She taught me about God, through my Sunday school classes, mentored me as a youth growing up, and a dear friend that praise for me. I could not have asked God to place a better person in my life. I would also like to give a special thank you to Janet Milton for being my second editor, great friend, and mentor. She is always uplifting. She undoubtedly believes in me oftentimes more than I believe in myself. Lastly, I want to thank all my family and friends who support me in all my endeavors. I can be exhausting at times; however, your love and support never fails.

FOREWORD

As I began to write this foreword, my mind went literally back to the future. It went back to the formative years of the author and envisioned the future which God has already prepared for her. Being an author of one book and a contributing writer in another, I understand the creative process and courage needed to write from an introspective perception. This is what Charmion did. What a timely title and focus: "Drowning, You Can't Breathe Water! – How I Survived." This has nothing to do with the social drama of today and political activism in our time. I can't breathe is an insightful, transparent, honest inward look at the impact decisions have made on her life. This reading made me examine my life and analyze choices in life I made or let others make for me. This is what Charmion does in this reading. It will review the process of discovery, impact of decisions, disguised depression, and reaching your destination. Charmion is well equipped to write this. I watched this young lady through the lenses of being her pastor, begin the journey as an energetic child, who became an enthused teen, who grew into an example setting young adult, who now is writing as an example of honesty for all adults. This is what makes this book an entertaining yet enlightening read for all.

Here is what we find. Charmion reveals the process of discovery. It was a painful yet priceless journey. In this book she will synoptically show how she went through discovering herself, her purpose, her passion, and finally her God. This is a must-read section for all who are seeking their own path.

You learn that discovery will aid in determining your destination. Do you or have you considered where God is leading you in your life? Charmion discovers her destination and honestly records the associated uncertainty. I knew the end goal but the pathway and roads to get there remained unclear to her as well as us. In an epic film it is said, "when you don't know where you are going, any road will take you there." Well, imagine when you see your destination but remain unsure of the road! This is what she reveals in her life. As a result, you will find in her zeal to prove herself, she spent countless hours disguising the truth. When will we step in and admit where we are?

With truth in focus, she now moves us to decision time and process. A question is raised:" Will you live or die?" The key premise here in this section is that all questions leave us with a choice. The Bible says, "Choose ye this day!" What Charmion reveals is life is a choice and she either made her choice or worse allowed choices for her life to be made by others. How many of us are where we are today because of choices made by others for us? An additional powerful point made is doing nothing is also a choice in life. What captivated me is where she reveals when one is going through life depression is inevitable to all. Yet never forget, depression is a choice as well. This is where the book will spend great effort in examining how honest with the reader Charmion is about her journey. She will reveal her weaknesses and character faults that became strengths when refocused.

Finally, she completes the process with learnings. I heard an old song in a movie:" I'm Singing in The Rain." This is what Charmion learned, how to sing in the rain. As a result, we will discover singing and thinking will turn negativism into positive outlooks that bring joy. Find your joy and you find your peace. Find your peace and wow, I Can Breathe! Follow your dream with realistic goals then you can live, learn, and lead. Enjoy the read and live the outcomes.

Larry G. Mills Th.D.

CONTENTS

THE BACKSTORY	1
THE BIG DECISION	5
DESTINATION ATLANTA	9
DAYS IN LIFE	17
DROWNING	25
DECIDE: LIVE OR DIE?	29
CLEAN HOUSE AND TRASH IT	37
LET IT GO	45
DO NOT WORRY	51
SMILE AND CHOOSE HAPPINESS	55
TRAIN YOUR MIND	61
SING A SONG	67
GET ACTIVE	71
THE WHY	75
FIND YOUR PEACE	87
CONCLUSION	97

INTRODUCTION

Depression kills people. It's a fact. The number of suicidal attempts is great in number, however, the attempts which do not fail result in death. This is a sad reality. Especially when all you hear about the person is how they seemed to have everything in order, how they had so much going for them, how they always had a smile on their face, how they always helped everyone, took care of everyone, was the go-to person for advice, and one of the best people you could ever meet.

People are baffled at the thought this person took their own life. The questions from family members and close friends are very similar. What was so bad? How did I not know they were going through such a hard time? Why did they not come to me? I cannot answer for them. I can only tell my story.

I was the one that was jovial, people loved, over achiever, entrepreneur, go getter, the life of the party, and the one with the big smile. You would never fathom I would be going through a depression. I had reached a point where the weight of the world took over and led me into a deep depression. Although I never considered taking my life, had I not recognized it was depression who knows if that would have been my ending point.

I wrote this book to walk you through a portion of my life that led me into a depressive state. I uncover how I recognized it and provide steps and tools used that helped me through my depression.

If you are the one person people call on for help, gives good advice, people rely on, always the person to bail you out, always the person to figure things out, expected to be in charge and run everything, handles everything in your life and the lives of everyone dear to you, you might be drowning and don't even know it.

If you have the weight of the world on your shoulders this book is for you. If you know someone that is always the person people rely on, that always come through, always have a smile on their face, always helping people, share this book. It could save their life. Depression kills because you can't breathe water. This book is the life jacket.

The Backstory

Before college, I really wrestled with which degree I should obtain. Should it be a performing arts degree or business degree? Well, my mom made the decision for me. She said I needed to focus on a degree that I could fall back on in case this acting thing did not work. That was probably one of the worst decisions I ever made. You live, and you learn. I would tell anyone to follow his/her dream. It is what wakes you up in the morning and gives you the motivation you need to keep going. The only key to following your dream is to be realistic about it. Set standards and goals that are achievable. Have a backup plan that is based on your dream. I could have very well obtained a performing arts degree. If by chance things did not go as planned, I could have been an instructor. I could have started a small theatre company or quite literally, a large theatre company. The sky is the limit, right? These are the type of back up plans that should have been in place. Not something that is completely different from my dreams and aspirations, which was obtaining a degree in Business Economics from Florida Agricultural and Mechanical University. Go Rattlers!

Before completing my four years of college, I had my first and only son. As a single parent, the words of my mother telling me to obtain what she called was a meaningful, solid, and secured degree was now laying heavy on my mind. I had to consider someone else now. My son needed security; so, I continued to pursue and accomplish that degree in Business Economics without regret. Was she right? She was not.

This was a life lesson I will now pass on to others. In my mom's defense, that's what she knew. She was only telling me this based on her experiences and life lessons. Yet as the old saying goes, to know better is to do better. You do not have to only learn from your own mistakes; learn from the mistakes of others. It could very well save you a lot of time and effort.

After college and years of working in the corporate arena, I walked away and decided to follow my lifelong dream and move away from home. I moved to Seattle after my current job was going out of business. Seattle was a place where I was able to learn and grow in the theatre arena. All I wanted to do was act. I loved being on stage, and if anyone is familiar with Seattle, it is definitely a theatre town. On every corner you can find a stage. If you love acting and plays, you could attend one every weekend, from the small intimate theatres to the big box theatres, and I loved it.

While in Seattle, I was receiving the training I needed through classes. I was also receiving the practice I needed by performing on stage. This was the life I wanted. If I was not acting, I was training. If I was not training, I was teaching children to act, and this was great! My plan was to get the training and experience I needed in Seattle and head to L.A. to make it big. I felt like I was well on my way, and nothing could stop me now. Everything was falling into place, and I was finally doing what I wanted to do.

Drowning

The only thing I did not love about Seattle was the weather. It really took some getting used to. When comparing the two, bad weather and living my dream, hands down on the life of pursuing my dream prevailed. Then I gave it all up for what I thought was the greater good for my son. I had a BIG decision to make.

The Big Decision

My son's father at the time signed a big contract from his employer and decided to be very generous and help me purchase a new home. The story is a little complicated. To keep it short, I could have either used the money then which could only go towards the purchase of a house or taken a chance at losing the money if I had waited for the next opportunity. In all reality waiting for the next opportunity was equivalent to losing the money for the down payment all together. There was no guarantee the money would be there down the line if I decided to wait. Well, I am not crazy, I took advantage of my offer and placed a large down payment on my home for my son and me.

The big decision I had to make was the location of this home. Would it be in Seattle where I am living out the first part of my goal to become a famous actress by obtaining the skills and training I need? Should it be in L.A. to begin my second phase of my career path and try to tap into television? Or Orlando, where all my family lives, where the housing market was indeed a lot more affordable, and where my son would grow up around family? Moving to Orlando would also provide additional support needed as a single parent.

Well with that list I did what a good mother would do, I decided to move back home to Orlando, Florida. The move back was ok. Again, it was not a decision based on my dreams and goals in life. I based it on what I felt was the normal unselfish thing to do. It was natural. I did not think at that time I was putting my son before my dreams and happiness. I just thought it was the best decision for the both of us. If it was better for him, it was better for me. Making him happy was making me happy, at least I thought. Right? Wrong, because I got off track when I put my son before myself. I moved from Seattle, Washington after being there for about 3 years because I did not want this opportunity to purchase a house to pass me by. I chose Orlando thinking about the best life for my son and gave up my dream and my goal in life.

When I moved back to Orlando and purchased my home, I was around my family and friends again, so the compromise and sacrifice did not seem too great. However, it turned out to be massive. I had the acting and theatre bug in me and there was nothing big going on in Orlando. I researched and signed up for classes and some of the so-called legitimate acting schools. Classes were a joke. I was literally in them saying to myself, "I could teach a better class". When they would ask me to spend a tremendous amount on headshots and not send me on casting calls, I really felt like Orlando was a joke. It screamed scam, and unfortunately 90% of the students in the class did not know it. I had to weed out all the bad schools and find the legitimate ones. I finally secured an agent, thank God, still it took some time, and I was introduced to legitimate agencies and schools. I did some commercial acting, very little theatre, webisodes, and a sitcom; however, that was on a small scale to me. I wanted more, and the opportunities were limited.

While dealing with the entertainment arena in Orlando, I was introduced to writing sitcoms and loved it as well. This made me even more hungry for the entertainment industry. The very first sitcom I wrote was a webisode called "Miserably Single". Go figure! Yep, based on a few girlfriends that were trying hard to connect with men. It is cute and funny to say the least. I am biased because I am the writer.

Now I had the acting bug and writing bug and no platform to express it in the capacity to be successful. After 4 years of this, I was done with Orlando and could not wait to get out. I thought about it long and hard and did not know what to do. Should I move again? Should I give up on my dream and take another path? I did not want to give up just yet on my dream, so I created a plan and was going to move to Atlanta.

Atlanta, the next up and coming Hollywood, was only 6 hours away, close to family, and would afford a lot of opportunity. I told myself when my son graduates from high school, I am leaving. I am packing my bags when I pack his bags for college. I told myself this for 3 additional years. My son and mom heard me repeat this constantly. I am sure they were tired of listening. I sacrificed those 3 years to avoid ripping him from family, his high school, and friends. So, when that day came, I left. They could not believe it. I moved to Atlanta to pursue my career in acting, and I was super excited.

Destination Atlanta

I moved in with my cousin in Atlanta. He was a tremendous help because I really did not know anything about the city beyond me visiting multiple times for the FAMU classic. Living with my cousin gave me the opportunity to venture out and see where it would be best for me to live long term and get my life situated without the initial heavy moving cost. Everything was falling in place for me again, and for the second time, I was overwhelmed with joy in starting my career in entertainment. I secured an agent after a few months, and I was well on my way; at least I thought. I was auditioning and not getting cast at all. Either the competition was great, or my acting skills had gotten rusty or both. All I know is I was not booking crap. The *only* reason I moved to Atlanta was to act and write. This was not happening at all. I knew where there were more opportunities in the entertainment industry there would also be more competition. I did not know it would be this difficult. Atlanta was becoming the new Hollywood, and I was here trying to make it happen. Not booking a job equaled not making any money. Well, we all know what that means. I did not have a huge savings, and it was not looking good to say the least. I really thought I was going to live off my acting career. Do not laugh. I was serious. I was completely unrealistic, but I was serious.

I thought my savings would cover me until I booked my next gig. Well, a year later without booking any acting gigs my savings account was constantly diminishing. Clearly, I had a lot more confidence in myself than the casting directors in Atlanta. I was not getting any acting jobs; so, I had to find a regular job, and that was challenging.

Being in the entertainment business, employment is hard because you must find something that pays the bills and provides a flexible schedule. This is because you should be available at any moment for an audition. In trying to do this I found myself working for a lot of scammers. I did not know Atlanta was known for scamming. It was so bad I had one of my checking accounts closed for a fraudulent check. After getting ripped off and working for companies who never paid me, my funds were looking low. I seemed to find jobs with all the owners that did not know how to run their business. I was clearly not a good judge of character when it came to that. I needed money. Paying bills became my focus. I had to survive. I literally forgot about acting because I had to focus on providing a roof over my head.

Instead of looking for ONE job that secured me financially, I took on several flexible jobs which left me no time for acting. I auditioned here and there; nevertheless, focus and motivation were not there. At one point I found myself just working and not pursuing my dream. Since this was happening, I was getting tired and frustrated. I did not know what to do; so, I just worked. I hated every minute of it. The bills were paid; however, I was not doing what I dreamed of doing. I was not making moves to accomplish my goals in life. The money was there. The fulfilment was not. I felt incomplete even though the financial stress was eliminated. I was just working and paying the bills. This seems normal for most people. I was not normal. I did not want the normal life. I wanted to be the one that reached her goal and dream in life. I wanted to be the one that did not settle because life was ok. I wanted to fulfill my dream. Not working towards that goal made me feel like something was missing all the time. It made me feel lonely. I was single at the time, so I started dating and met my guy. The relationship was a breath of fresh air. It gave me an outlet and stress release from everything I was dealing with at the time. Now I had a new relationship, which distracted me from feeling so lonely and unfilled because I was not reaching my goal.

Since the finances from working multiple jobs were ok, I decided I should move out of my cousin's place into my own space. I was thinking this would at least make me feel like I had accomplished something. So, I found a place and was on my own. It was time, and I felt good about it. Even with this great feeling, the move did not do it for me.

I was not being fulfilled with the things I had set out for myself. I was not walking in my destiny. I was not living the life I pictured for myself. I thought I had finally gotten back on track moving to Atlanta to pursue acting again. Where was it leading me? I put myself first and was thinking this is finally my time to do what I want to do again. It was at a time in my life where I had little responsibility. My son was away at college and his room and board, and his major necessities were covered. Again, nothing that I wanted was happening for me.

If that was not enough, my agent called me and said he was releasing me from my contract. I was not really surprised, just extremely disappointed. I really had already given up on my acting career and put it on the back burner. I guess they noticed it as well and released me. Why would the agency keep me? I was not making them any money because I was not booking any roles. I also never called to keep in touch and make sure I was on the roster. They probably thought I had given up as well.

At this moment I had concluded that I should take a break from acting altogether. I was not focused on it, and now that I was no longer represented by an agent, what was the point? Could I even secure another agent? How long would that take? Maybe this was not what I was supposed to be doing. Just take a break and work were thoughts that consumed my mind. I thought if I just stopped everything else and just worked, it would give me the capital I needed to stack some money. When I did decide to return to the entertainment industry, I would not have any financial concerns. It would at the very least alleviate the stress of paying my bills when I started back on the track of pursuing my dream of acting. Also, since I no longer had an agent, the stress of me not booking any roles would also be eliminated.

The next battle would be saving up enough money as quickly as I could. Because I had my own place now, the amount of money I could save was not as substantial as before. Living expenses had almost tripled. Although I could afford it, I just could not save as much as I was saving before. I needed to find something that would provide more income in a timely manner. The longest I wanted to take a break from acting was only 6 months, a year at best.

So, I decided on the additional job, and I did what many people do in Atlanta, real estate investing.

I dove headfirst in real estate investing. I chose this because it would give me the lump sum I needed at the end of the deal to get ahead on my finances. Because of the nature of the business, I still had to work because you do not make money while you are rehabbing. The money comes after the sale. So, I started a small business doing kitchen and cabinet designs. Since I was in the property renovation arena, I thought it could not hurt to capitalize on a needed commodity as well. I also started driving for Uber. I was all over the place. I was so busy and so overwhelmed with trying to juggle it all. Once the other projects were complete, I did not take on anymore. I just wanted to finish my project, make the money, and go back to pursing my dream. If that was not enough, I lost a big cabinet contract and had to cover a huge loss when one of my installs went bad. Between me being extremely busy with managing my own rehab project, not securing additional properties to manage, cabinet installers screwing up a client's kitchen with cabinet installations, and me having to replace cabinets from my pocket, I was back at square one waiting for my investment house to sell. No cabinet jobs and no more managing properties meant no income coming in. All I had now was the proceeds coming from the house that I was renovating which was still a few months away from being complete.

This was breaking me down. I had nothing. My stress also put strain on my relationship with my boyfriend. What started out as a breath of fresh air was turning into a smoke-filled room from a bad cigar smell. I felt like my world was ending. I just told myself that I must keep going.

In the meantime, I started living off my credit cards. Bad idea again by the way. I just felt like I had no other choice. Now my credit cards were maxed out, and I still had no money coming in. My boyfriend covered the day-to-day bills, such as rent, electric and cable in the midst of a shaky relationship. He had moved into my place; and he really did not mind covering the cost, even in the midst of it all. I also had personal bills like my car insurance, health insurance, cell phone bill, and credit card bills. I wanted to do more for myself, but I could not. I really did not want his extra help as badly as I needed it. With the stress I was dealing with and other personal things, the relationship was falling apart. We could not seem to agree on anything, and I was beginning to put my stress on him. I do not know if I realized we did not have as much in common as I thought we did or maybe it was the stress I was dealing with at the time. I knew when we met it was a breath of fresh air because I needed a mental break from the regular routine. I needed something different. He was different. He was fun. He took my mind off my current situation. I did not look at commonalities, values, beliefs, goals etc. I looked at the relationship as something that gave me a sense of happiness at the time. When things get tough is when you start to see a person for who they really are. He started to see me, and I started to see him. I needed someone to lean on, to talk through my troubles, to encourage me through my pain and failure and he was not that guy. He was not a communicator. He did not like to talk. He avoided confrontation at all costs. He could not counsel me through my hard times. He did not understand my stress. He could not be my savior. Was he supposed to be? My expectations were too great for any human! I expected him to do something no one could. I expected him to be something he could never be. This pushed him away and made things vastly different between us. The love he had for me was different now. I did this to him. I did this to us and could not change it.

I would sit in church on multiple Sundays just crying because I felt like I was flat lining. My life was out of control, and I did not know where to turn or what to do. I was ready to throw in the towel. I had already put my dream on hold. I had already decided to take a break from the stress of it all. I was more stressed out than before. I stopped pursuing my dream and for what? To still be stressed out! This was supposed to be easier! I was supposed to be taking a mental and emotional break from the stress I was getting from pursuing my dream. I had prayed to God several times to show me if Atlanta was where I needed to be. If it was Atlanta, then show me what I should be doing as well. I prayed and prayed, and God spoke to me through a sermon, and it was so clear to me. He told me, "Stop praying. All you are doing is praying, and I heard you the first time. All you do is pray, pray, pray. You need to trust me. Trust that I have your back and move. Move away from those things that make you unhappy and unproductive and reach toward those things that I have placed before you." Whew! That was deep and eye opening. I knew what I had to do. I think I went to the extreme because I let go of almost everything. Shoot, in my opinion everything had me unhappy and unproductive. I also broke up with my boyfriend. I did a complete clean. I think I did it so drastically because I had no other choice. The emotional state I was in forced me to just do it and do it now.

After this clean sweep, I went back home to Orlando to visit to clear my head. My family and friends were there for emotional support, and I just needed an escape after I broke from this drastic change.

Days in Life

While at home visiting in Orlando, I decided to attend one of my close girlfriend's church. The service was awesome and just what I needed. The praise and worship songs were uplifting and encouraging, and the message for that day was excellent. The preacher spoke about it being the year to hear; basically, she said to listen to what God is saying to us and act on that. I failed to mention that God has told me several times that I am not focused. I have too much going on, and I need to focus on what is important. After the message, the preacher extended an invitation for the congregation to come forward for prayer. I was very emotional at the time because of my recent past situation. I still was at a standstill without direction. I was waiting on my next direction from God. He told me to move and clean house, and I did that. Now what? While I had my reservation about praying for the same things, I was waiting on the next step or answer from God, and this seemed like the next best platform. I went up to the front with several others who had come for many different reasons. What I did not know was the pastor's husband was going to prophesy to me. He told me he saw writing in my future. He said I needed to write. WOW! I had been asking God to show me my purpose in life, and it was to write. When he said writing, it hit me like a ton of bricks. I started crying out to God and saying, "Thank you". I was praising God so much and crying so hard when I received that breakthrough. People were probably looking at me crazy. I was in the moment. Everyone that had come up front for prayer had left and gone back to their seats. I was still crying out to the Lord and thanking him for what he had done and revealed to me. I do not know how long I was up there alone. Keep in mind I was a visitor. I knew how I looked at visitors at my church who came up to the front for prayer, falling all out, crying, carrying on, and extending the service because they could not compose themselves. This particular Sunday, it was me. I have since changed my view of course. ☺ One lady came up to me after service and said, "You tried to get all the blessing today for yourself, didn't you?" I looked at her with a sincere smile and laughed, "I sure did, and I needed it."

So now leaving church I was excited. I felt like more weight had been lifted, and I knew what I needed to do, write. Writing would be my purpose in life. Although I had written things in the past; I never considered myself a writer. I really only wrote things before out of need. I needed to pass my class. I needed to write a script so I could act in a sitcom or webisode. Growing up; I wrote songs because that's how I connected with my twin. He played the piano, and I sang. I was creative; so, I wrote songs, and he created the music. This was one of the only things my brother enjoyed doing with me. He was a boy, and I did not want to play his games, and he did not want to play mine. I did not write for any other reason. The lingering question in my mind was, "What should I write?" After pondering over this revelation, it became less strange to me. Writing was my purpose. It does come easy for me when I do it.

I already had ideas of things to write when I caught the writing bug years ago. There was a list of writings and ideas saved on my computer. I let those ideas sit because at the time that's not what I saw in my future. Why I kept or created the list at the time was not as clear. It was now. I also had a few great storylines for movies I had been sitting on. I had written a few songs. I had started a few plays and never finished. Even before the writing confirmation, I had told myself I needed to write a book about my journey in life. The book was just a task that I figured I would tackle after I made it to the top as an actress. It was something I saw myself writing on vacation to kill time after I accepted the award for best actress. I am sure you are laughing again at my thought process, as you should.

Well, I continued the day with a few of my girlfriends; we ate, played games, pantomimed to songs, ate again, and laughed a lot. This was a good day, and I had some peace and clarity. I had walked away from baggage and weight that was pulling me down, and I was clear on my purpose in life. This moment in my life was like no other. I was well on my way to doing what I was created to do and was ready. I just wanted to write. Because this journey was so fresh. I decided to work on this book first. I got a good night's rest and was ready to take on the world with my writing.

The very next day was a bit stressful. I knew writing was what I needed to do. Everything around me was preventing me from doing it. My mom needed me to do something; then it was my auntie; then one of my girlfriends unexpected visit took up almost my entire day. When I noticed this was happening, I started to feel disappointed in myself. I started feeling like a failure again. Some of those same feelings I had back in Atlanta were trying to resurface. I had a clear direction for my life, and I was not able to focus. I had just let everything go and knew my path in life, but I could not start writing. This was one day that I should have been overwhelmed with joy, but I was not. I was finally on the road to my destiny, and I started to stress out again. I was thinking this could not be happening. I still had some healing to do from letting everything else go. Although the destination of where my life was headed was clear, the road was not. The weight and cares of the world had just dropped off my shoulders, and I was trying to get my strength back. I was still weak. I just wanted to be great. I just wanted to write. I wanted to see how I would feel if I just did what I was created to do. I had received confirmation on my purpose in life. I had received my answer, and I could not even do it on the first day. I took a step back and allowed myself to just breathe. I was determined not to have these stressful feeling again; so, I just let it go, I just relaxed, and told myself to start tomorrow. I did just that. It took the stress away, and I enjoyed the rest of the evening.

The next morning, I got up early, I wanted to get a good start before anyone could interrupt me. I pulled out my laptop and just started typing. The words were just flowing. My mom finally woke up. I wanted her to go back to sleep so I could continue my writing uninterrupted. All that, "Good Morning." "How are you doing?" "Are you still writing?" "What are you writing?" "How's it going?" Her questions were just enough to interrupt my writing flow. Then I noticed the time. I was so focused I did not know I had been typing for 2 hours straight. It felt like 30 minutes. I could not believe it. I was proud of myself.

While I was still visiting family, I continued to write over the next week or so. I did most of it early in the morning because this turned out to be the best uninterrupted time of the day. Writing was refreshing. It gave me a since of peace. It was something I could do for hours that only seemed like minutes. I never seemed bored with writing or obligated to do it. It was not like a chore. It was satisfying to the point where I felt like if I was not doing it, I felt weird. I felt incomplete when I was not writing. This was "writing" for me. I wrote everyday while in Orlando, and it became my routine.

My short vacation came to an end. Back to Atlanta I went. Feeling a little weird because although I had let things go and dropped everything when I left Atlanta, I still had to clean up the situation with my now ex-boyfriend. I also had to determine my employment options. I was no longer looking for acting gigs or multiple streams of income because all I needed now was a job to pay my bills and time to write. Well, to fast forward, my boyfriend never left, and the relationship continued to be incredibly challenging to say the least.

I also went back to what I knew best with the side jobs because I was so used to being an entrepreneur and not working for people. Before long I was not writing at all. I was not writing because I was so stressed. I could not focus. When I wanted to write the words were no longer flowing. I would start typing and all I could think about were the issues and problems I was having. I had reverted to the same lifestyle with small odd jobs that were barely paying the bills again, and I was in an unhealthy relationship. I could not focus; so, I started working on creating a card game instead. I know what you are thinking. "Where did that come from?" I had so many things on my bucket list; they would surprise you. I had so many ideas for new products, they would amaze you. This is one major reason I could not focus. I focused on the card game because I was so stressed out, I needed to do something that would give me a since of accomplishment when I completed it. My thoughts were that I would sell the card game for income and write. Once I started writing I would be fine again. This was another big idea that I had planned all out. I did accomplish it. I did all the artwork, created the rules, designed each card, and got it all produced ready to sell. I received a lot of good reviews on the game. This created an optimism that my plan was going to work.

I ordered 3000 units and sold about 300. This was not the plan. Now, I have all these playing cards to sell with another credit bill. I was back to square one AGAIN. My life was spinning out of control. I felt low; I did not want to eat; then I wanted to eat everything. I could not sleep. I isolated myself from friends. I was like a zombie. I cried often, and sometimes I did not think I could stop. I could not talk to my boyfriend. I needed to be strong for my family and my son, so all the energy I did have was used to pretend that everything was ok. I was not ok. I was falling apart, and the fact that I had clear direction made it even more difficult to cope. I could see a future of happiness and peace. It just was not within reach. My future was dangling in front of me just teasing me, just barely out of reach. I was doing everything I knew to do, and it was never enough. I was at a low. I was slipping in a place that I had never experienced before. This place was far worse than the previous time. How could it be worse when I had discovered so much about myself. I was not sure. I was just sad all the time and did not care anymore. I was not motivated to do anything. Crying daily became my routine, and strangely enough, I accepted it.

I stayed in this low state for several months. This became a common place for me. I was drowning and barely functioning. I did not want to be defeated. I just did not think I was strong enough to win. All I was doing was letting each day go by. I would continue to pray to God and just thank him for letting me see another day. I would cry out to him and just sit and wait. I finally said enough is enough. I do not really know what made me snap out of it; at any rate I am glad I did. I was drowning, and I was the only person that could save me.

Drowning

One reason I used the term drowning, because it was exactly how I was feeling. I was drowning in disappointment, bad relationships, overdue bills, unaccomplished goals, an unhappy lifestyle, and issues and circumstances that just did not seem to fall in place. Every time I turned around, things were at the tip of changing. Nothing ever changed for me. It was disappointment knocking at my door all the time. I was exhausted beyond measure. It was all I could bare. Nothing else could happen, or I would literally die. I would drown in life's battles, circumstances, expectations, and unaccomplished goals, all while gasping for air and screaming for help.

    I was trapped in the wilderness just walking in circles. I had goals and dreams, and nothing was happening for me. On every end I felt like a failure. I wondered daily, "Why is this happening to me? What have I done or not done to deserve this life I am living? What am I doing wrong?" I pondered this consistently. I could never find an acceptable answer. I am a good person. I am loyal and caring to my family and friends. I help others more than I really can. I have a relationship with God, and I am highly active at my church. I consider myself to be a great mom. I treat others how I want to be treated at least 98% of the time because people can take you there, just being honest. I try to do the best I can. I consider myself to be productive and creative. The water of life that surrounded me just kept rising. The water continued to rise day by day, which turned to hour by hour. The rising water was tremendously overbearing especially for me who could barely swim in the first place. Before I knew it the only part of my face that was out of the water was my nose and a small portion of my upper lip. Take a moment and imagine that. Just my nose and upper lip were out of the water, and I was standing straight up on the tip of my toes. At that point I was completely motionless and afraid to move. If I moved, I would drown for sure because there was so much weight on my shoulders. As I mentioned, my weight was in the form of rejection, unaccomplished goals, bad relationships, financial struggles, and feeling like a failure. I wanted to cry. My heart was hurting; my mind was spinning, and no one was around to save me. At this point I could not cry anymore because I was afraid the tears would cover the only part of my body that was unsubmerged. I just stood there standing and trying to hold it together hoping that a little sunshine would come my way. If the sun would shine just a little, it would evaporate some of the water to give me more time to figure out this thing called life. The sun did not shine, and I could not take it anymore. The uncontrollable tears begin to flow, and before long I was completely covered with water. I was drowning. All I could do was pray. "Lord save me! Please God, save me!" That sincere cry out to God changed my life and gave me what I needed to survive.

Drowning

My life was at a place where I needed something to happen, and it needed to happen now. I mean right now. I was trapped and consumed with things I needed to walk away from. I did not know where to go. I was all out of options; however, there was a decision that needed to be made. I did not want to die. Although death for me was not literal or equivalent to suicide, my death would come in the form of not living a whole and healthy life. Instead of a life full of joy and happiness, a life of peace and contentment, a life of love; my life depicted the opposite. I had nothing left inside of me. I had no other choice. I had to decide. Stay in the water or get out? Live or die? I got out and I decided to live. Will you live or die?

Decide: Live or Die?

One must ask themselves, "Will I live or die?" It seems like a simple answer. No one chooses to die, right? Wrong, many people unfortunately have chosen this path every day. They allow life circumstances to get the best of them. They feel like there is nothing better than death, and they give up. Sometimes the choice is literally where they take their own life. Other times it is just living day to day in a state of mourning and non-movement. This was my life.

I was at my final hour, and it was either stay and drown or get out the water. Well, I got out. What did that look like? What did that mean? I made a choice that whatever was holding and weighing me down, I was not going to allow it to control me any longer. I allowed the things that were weighing me down to have power over me. I was not where I wanted to be in life, and I allowed that to make me feel like I was not good enough. I allowed the fact that I was not walking into my destiny make me feel like a failure. I allowed the loss of income and not being able to pay my bills on time create mental thoughts that I was not a responsible person. I allowed myself to stay in an unhealthy relationship because I blamed myself for not being patient or understanding. I was not perfect; so why should I expect more from my mate. This is what I told myself consistently. I convinced myself that I did not deserve better. I convinced myself that I should do more. I conditioned myself to believe the reason I was in a state of depression was because I did something wrong. I was being punished. That's the incorrect mindset. No one is perfect, and I did deserve better. I deserve to be happy and have peace. I deserve it because I am special. "I am fearfully and wonderfully made" (***Psalm 139:14***). I am the head and not the tail. I will always be at the top and never the bottom (***Deuteronomy 28:13***). I have a peace with God that surpasses all my understanding (***Philippians 4:7***). I will take you through my journey of how I made it through and how I defeated this enemy called depression.

Depression is a CHOICE! Brace yourself and mark my words. It is a harsh reality. It is true, and no one wants to say it. No one wants to accept this responsibility. When I breakdown the root cause of my depression, you will agree. I had to really think back on things that were going on in my life: the good and the bad; the day-to-day operation; how it all started; what I went through; how things progressed, and how they fell apart. I had to analyze my emotions and my thoughts. Pondering over all this made me determine that I had chosen a state of lowness. I had chosen to feel anxious and moody. I had chosen to give up. I had chosen to accept I was a failure, and I would never accomplish my dream. I had chosen these things, this life.

Have you chosen to be depressed? Your immediate response would simply be, "Who on earth would choose to be depressed?" My immediate and candid response, "You". If you have ever been depressed, it is something that you have chosen. You may not agree at this moment. Just open your mind and your heart in defeating this choice that has been made. It is all on you. You should accept the responsibility. You have done this to yourself. You have created in your mind that you do not deserve better. You have allowed yourself to accept defeat and not to move forward. You have decided that you will never be great and that things are too hard. You have decided that whatever life throws your way you must take it and allow it to define you. This is the reality and an awfully hard pill to swallow. No doctor wants to tell a dying patient it is their fault they are dying when the underlying issue was something they could have avoided. Just like no one wants to say you have chosen to be in a state of sadness, lowliness, and self-worthlessness. It is not a genuinely nice thing to say, we can all agree. No one really likes cut and dry people who do not have filters on their mouths. People are so "nice-conscious" they do not want to tell you the truth. I have never had that problem. I agree that it is a bit insensitive. It goes to the old saying of kicking someone when they are already down. My thoughts are, if they are already down, they cannot get any lower. So, you might as well give it all to them at their lowest. At least then, when they get ready to overcome and fight, they know everything they are up against. Let me provide you with an example.

Does it drive you crazy when you are working on a project and out of the blue someone adds a missing element to your workload that needs to be incorporated before your task is complete? It would have been better to know everything you must tackle upfront than to find out midway through that there's more work to be done before the completion of the project.

This could be something as simple as traveling to a destination. Wouldn't you want to know the roadblocks ahead before you start? Wouldn't it be nice to know there will be 90% chance of rain before you arrive on your beach vacation? Wouldn't it be nice to know if there are roadblocks or closures ahead?

It could also be something as simple as making oatmeal raisin cookies. You thought you only needed oatmeal, raisins, and sugar at best. Although you want the homemade cookies, you do not want to put the effort in making them. Once you have placed in your mind to tackle the task, you discover you do not have the flour you need to complete it. You've pulled out all the ingredients and set time aside to make the cookies. In order for you to complete the cookie you must make a trip to the store. Now you are frustrated because additional time is required. This additional piece of missing information, although requires additional effort to accomplish the task at hand, would have been handled a lot better if all the information had been given at once. Had you known flour was needed, it would have been purchased prior to attempting the task.

Missing information can also result in incompletion. Would you rather spend time putting a zig saw puzzle together, working hard to achieve a finished product, just to find out the middle pieces of the puzzle are missing? Would you rather have all the pieces at once before tackling the project? This work could turn out to be in vain because you do not have all the pieces. The puzzle will never be complete. You have worked hard to achieve something without every component, and failure sets in. There is no way to complete this without all the missing pieces.

Accepting responsibility is a big piece of life's troubles and mishaps. I was always the straight shooter. I was concerned that if it were too soft, you would miss the point; so, I just laid it all out without filter. I left no room to read between the lines. I just gave the harsh flat-out truth. The truth sometimes hurts, and it is necessary. If you are depressed, the truth is, you did it to yourself. The good news is because it is a choice, you do not have to be depressed any longer. Many are thinking, "Wow that is a rude and cruel thing to say." Yes, it is a harsh reality.

Now do not confuse depression with being born with a physical illness. Do not confuse it with losing a job or a loved one. Do not confuse it with getting into a car accident and totaling your car. Do not confuse it with having a bad relationship or marriage. These things are called life. Life happens. Depression is a choice we make because these things are happening around us.

Although depression is a choice, depression is real. Depression can enter your life without you knowing it. Once it is there, it will take over, and it can be an extremely difficult process to get rid of it if you do not recognize it. Depression can become a routine like it did for me. I felt like I was in a state of mourning. Once I recognized it was depression, it validated my current feelings. Depressed people are sad. They feel low and want to be isolated. I accepted these feelings because in my mind it validated not only my situation, but it also validated my depression. I told myself that I should be depressed with everything that I was going through. I was supposed to be sad because my goals were not being achieved. I should be stressed out because I could not pay my bills. With everything that I was dealing with I should have been depressed, right? No! Why be depressed over things that depression itself cannot help? Will being depressed help?

Let's look at being depressed based upon goals not being achieved. Are you sad and depressed because you feel like a failure? If you are a failure that means you have stopped. You can only fail if you stop trying. If you have not stopped trying, you have not failed. Now what? So, you have stopped? Well, if you have stopped that was a choice to not keep going. You decided to give up. It could have been for multiple reasons. Maybe it was not for you. It could have been the wrong time. It could have been too hard to overcome or not what you expected. If you have determined those things and stopped, why are you depressed? You chose to stop.

Sadness is understandable. Being sad is different from being depressed. Sadness will come and go, and it does not consume your life to the point where there's no movement. Sadness does not handicap you because it is an emotion. You can still operate when your emotions are up or down. Depression is a handicap that keeps you from moving and operating to the best of your ability. Depression is something that can be avoided. Choosing happiness must be practiced consistently to prevent it. It is not easy.

Depression is like weight gain. If you do not avoid the fat stuff and work out, the weight will pile on, and you will be fat before you know it. Happiness is something that we must practice to maintain our mental and emotional shape to ward off depression. Once you get in shape it is easy to maintain. It is just hard to get there. In fact, it can be extremely difficult at times depending on what this thing we call "life" happens. The key is acknowledging how powerful depression can be and building the strength to overcome and defeat it. Never give up even when things do not seem like they are looking brighter. There are brighter days ahead if you keep going.

The major thing about depression is that you must decide whether or not you are going to let it take over your life. Will you live or die? That's the first step. You must make a decision. The choice is yours, and it is just that simple. When you have a made-up mind and choose to live, you are on the road of recovery. You can't breathe water; so, decide to live or die.

The steps below are what I used to heal myself from the sickness of depression and become a better me. These steps are what I practice often to prevent that unwanted visitor. They are in no particular order. Each step is important. I encourage you to start today and choose to be permanently healed from depression. You are worth it, and you deserve it!

Clean House and Trash It

I do not know about you, yet there is something about a clean house. It is rejuvenating! It brings about a peace and a calmness. It allows the mind to relax because there is no clutter. Nothing is tucked away in drawers or hidden in a closet. If it is not needed, it is not there. Everything is in order and has its own space. Everything is clean and there is nothing to do so your mind is at rest.

There are several benefits when your mind is at rest. Most of us know the benefits rest has on the body. The main benefit is better health. We also know the issues that come with the lack of rest or sleep. When your mind can rest, you sleep better. When we are sleep deprived, many things happen within our bodies. Studies have shown that sleep deprivation can lead to weight gain, weaken immune system, higher risk of heart disease and high blood pressure to name a few. Outside of this it is awfully hard to focus when you are tired. You cannot function to the best of your ability without the proper rest. If you are half functioning, then you are accomplishing your task either inadequately or often times at a slower pace than usual. This path again leads to unnecessary stress we invite into our lives. To avoid this area of stress everything must be put in its proper place. If it is not needed it should be thrown out and put in the trash. This process might be the most time consuming to achieve. It will not be something that will happen overnight. In fact, it may take weeks, months or even a good year or two.

The thought of two years seems like an extremely long time. The time it takes depends on what you are cleaning. Compare someone who has a mansion to someone with a 2-bedroom apartment. The one with the apartment has a lot less cleaning to do if you only consider the size of the space. Some people have more space than others because of their lifestyle or obligations. Some have jobs that consume a lot of their time. Some have children, spouses, extracurricular activities, and parents to care for. All these things are items that take up space in our lives.

Using the analogy of house cleaning, how hard is it to mess up a room or space when there is hardly anything in it? Picture a walk-in closet. You have 5 jackets, 10 pair of pants, 15 tops and 10 sweaters. Your shoes consist of 10 pairs of all the basic styles and colors. There is a place for everything because a walk-in closet can clearly hold a lot more than 40 articles of clothing and 10 pairs of shoes. The only way this closet should be unclean is if you do not hang up your clothes and just dump the clothes on the floor. There is no reason you should not be able to step into your closet, select the items you will wear and keep moving to enjoy the day. When you have the basic needs and are not overconsumed with items, it is hard to mess it up.

Let us just say you had a bad morning. You woke up late and did not figure out what you were wearing the night before. You took a few things off the rack and left them there because your time was limited. You left the house with your closet out of order. Even though you had a bad morning and some things got out of whack, which can sometimes happen, it will not take long to get back on track. The bounce back will be easy because it is not overcrowded, and everything still has its place. All you need to do is hang the clothes back up and put them in their rightful location. The time it will take you to get back to a clean organized closet should be quick. Even if all the clothes were out of place, the bounce back would be short.

Now, on the other hand, say your closet is packed full of clothes, of which I am guilty. Pants are folded neatly, except you have stacks of 100 pairs of pants. Clothes are piled on racks all the way to the ceiling. You have too many shoe boxes with no room for one more pair. It is so packed that it is impossible to slide an article of clothing on the rack. Because your closet is neat, clean and color coordinated, you think you are good. Reality Check (News Flash), there are too many clothes.

Imagine someone broke into your house. They went through your clothes and took everything off the hangers and messed up your entire closet. How long will it take to get this closet back in order? This could take days and even weeks! Once you begin to get your closet back in order you realize there are clothes you have not worn in years. Some with tags still on them. You find things you cannot wear, will never wear or should not be wearing. If those things were removed and never there in the first place there would be less cleaning which means less recovery time.

Although the reference was the cleaning of a house, which may still be needed, the cleaning I am referring to is your personal life. What is occupying your life? What is taking up space? Just like the burglar, what has robbed your time and space that has you all out of order? This is directly related to your peace and happiness. Is it needed? Does it have its own space? Do you have things covering it up? Can you even see it?

Analyze your life and determine things to get rid of that is not needed that is taking up space in your life. Just because it is there, or it is in good condition does not mean you need it.

Just like the overcrowded closet, you may have too much stuff going on in your life with no space in between. Housecleaning needs to happen. Throw some stuff away. There are days that your life will be turned upside down. The less you must deal with when that happens determines the length of your recovery time.

When thinking of things that take up space or occupy most of our time, many list things like jobs, children, church, hobbies, side jobs, friends, and relationships. These are most common; at the same time, look at things like the energy we spend on being angry with someone. Every time I am angry with someone it is all I think about. I can hardly focus on my day. Even when I am busy doing something else, it is in the back of my mind. I cannot completely focus on what I am doing.

We also spend time daydreaming about things we have not accomplished, - meaningless phone conversations, hours spent on social media, or watching tv. All of these take up space in our lives.

Another thing we spend a lot of time on, which occupies our time, is being lazy. Sitting around doing nothing is unproductive. When nothing is being accomplished, there is a lack that is present. Depression stems from not being fulfilled or lacking something. What has your laziness prevented you from accomplishing?

Other things that consume time are trust, control, and patience. Do you have trouble trusting certain processes and procedures? Trusting others to do things for you? Trusting things will work out for the better. Do you want to control every situation in your life? Can you not just go with the flow? Being in control requires a lot of responsibility, and you should not want to control everything and everyone.

Are you patient? Do you expect others to move as quickly and efficiently as you? Can you allow things to take more time than needed? Are you stressed out if things are moving slower than what you would consider a normal pace? Impatient people tend to take over the situation to accomplish the task at hand.

If we are trying to live a life with less stress as possible, being overloaded with items we have no room for can trigger a sense of being overwhelmed. You must determine what is important to keep. The other stuff you should trash and declutter your life. It will only drown you. You can't breathe water no matter how hard you try. Toss it out. It is that simple.

Although simple, there are certain things that cannot be tossed out. If you have children, of course, you cannot throw them away, unless they are adults. Let us use them for an example because even things around your children can be trashed. What is it that you are doing for your child that they can do for themselves? Many of us take on responsibilities that our children should have for several reasons:

    1. We do not require them to take responsibility to do things. – Trust issues – Trash it!

    2. We want it done our way. – Control issues – Trash it!

    3. We want it completed fast. – Patience issues – Trash it!

These mistakes fill up space. Let your children complete things that are age appropriate. There is no reason for you to fold clothes for a teenager. There is no reason for you to clean your 7-year old's room. If they are old enough to take the toys out the box surely, they can put them back in the box. There is no reason a 10-year-old is not able to load a dishwasher after a meal. Trust they can learn as you have. Stop wanting to control exactly how towels are positioned back in the linen closet or that the spoon in the dishwasher was faced down and not up. Be patient and allow them to take longer to complete a task. It may take them 30 additional minutes to complete something. Why is that an issue? That's time you can spend for you.

Control issues can also happen in the workforce with management. Train your employees and stop micromanaging them. You have hired them to do a job. Let them do it. If the performance is inadequate, then your job would be to find a better employee. This should be your only responsibility. This seems harsh. Just do the one job you were hired to do, which is to manage. Don't do two jobs, which would be your job and their job. You are micromanaging. This is filling up unnecessary space. Trash it.

We also try to save the world. How can you save the world when you have not saved yourself? We jump to help other people when we do not have the space to do it. If you love helping others, as I do, you must first clean some space out in order to make room to help them. It goes back to, if your closet is already full, why are you still shopping? You need to remove some stuff before you purchase more.

Often times we do not even realize how busy and consumed we are on a day-to-day basis. Have you ever really sat down and looked at your daily schedule? Do you know how many hours in a day are devoted to duties, work, and others? How much time do you give yourself? Some things we cannot remove and others we can. Most of us cannot remove our jobs, taking care of family or certain commitments. What we can do is decrease our commitment within those platforms. Make a list and take an analysis of what is important and remove those things that are not. Declutter your life for a better you. It is that simple.

Let It Go

There were several different things that I needed to let go, and they were all tied to one specific thing. It defined me. It consumed how I viewed things in life. It shaped my personality and created a barrier of which I was unaware. At times it placed me in the middle of dry land, motionless with nowhere to go. It kept me feeling like a failure. It put unwanted pressure on others around me. It robbed me of happiness and contentment. What was this one specific thing? This thing was being a perfectionist. Some may smile and suggest that this is indeed a good thing. For me, not so much. I will explain why.

I do not have many favorite things because I always think things should be better. Nothing really satisfied me. I do not remember a time where I can reflect and say it was the greatest thing that ever happened to me. This was a hard pill to swallow because I did not think my perception of things had created a false sense of how life is supposed to be. I thought I wanted things to be better because we should all want to strive to be great. I thought being less than great was people not wanting to put forth the effort to do better. I thought it was because of their laziness and lack of drive. I understood mistakes happening; despite that, I did not accept failure. Failure to me was giving up and not trying again. Failure was accepting mediocre when greatness was right next door. Based on what? What I considered perfect and great? What I determined was good and acceptable? What I internalized to be something without flaws? I did not have those "favorite" things because they were not perfect in my mind. I was searching for something better all the time and did not even recognize it.

Also, I naturally worried about everything always being a certain way and stressed about the circumstance or situation not being flawless based on my standards. As a perfectionist, I wanted everything to run smoothly, professionally, orderly, and without flaws. If I planned an event, I needed all the staff to arrive on time and ready to take on their task. If I wanted everyone to wear pink and someone showed up in fuchsia, it took me to another level. If I were directing a play and you could not remember your mark after multiple rehearsals, I wanted to scream. If the music cues were two seconds late in one of my productions, I was asking the music director if he was asleep because the mark was missed.

Additionally, I am a creator, and everyone does not want to create. Everyone does not want to think outside the box. Others are content with just getting by as long as they do not have to exert more time or energy. Some people do not desire growth. They are good where they are and at peace with the way things are going. If they are happy being in a certain place, I should respect it and move forward.

Furthermore, I am overly analytical. You cannot tell me much that I do not question. This does not mean I think you do not know what you are talking about. I just like to break things all the way down. I prefer to explore all options. I expected others to do the same.

Lastly, I was, what some would describe as, the professor. I thought it was my duty to teach people what they did not know. This literally drove me insane when people lacked common sense, were unruly, or acted as if they were raised in the wild. If a child was crying uncontrollably in public, I was the individual approaching the child's parent and explaining it is not ok to just let your child scream in public. I also took it a step further and asked the child what the problem was. If a cashier returned me the inappropriate amount of money, I took the time to teach them how to count the money back so it would not happen again. If I asked someone a direct question and they answered me with a broad statement, I was adamant about receiving a direct answer. If a person said they were going to commit to something and did not, I was livid. I did everything in my power to be a great person, follow the rules, do the right things, and help others. That's all I expected in return. When I did not get it, I was greatly disappointed, hurt and often stressed out. If I would go the extra mile and bend over backward for you, then you should do the same for me. This was not the case.

One would think I was perfect or nearly perfect. I made mistakes daily. I was not better than anyone else. I considered myself to be an average, sound minded, responsible person. I just expected everyone around me to perform on my level or better. If I could do it, you could do it. It was not rocket science. It was being a responsible, mature, and considerate adult. This was the average thing to do. It is the considerably, basic thing to expect from average, regular, everyday people.

Who wears clothes and does not know how to wash them? Who eats every day and does not know how to cook? Who works at a job and never learns the process and procedures? Who mistreats people, and does not expect to be mistreated? Who expects to be in a trusting and loving relationship when he or she does not show love or cannot be trusted? Who expects to be the leader and does not have the skills to lead? Who breaks the law and does not expect to be punished? Who expects much for little in return? The answer is A LOT of people. People I cannot control. People I cannot change. People who do not want to change. And people who are not perfect. Let it go! You can't breathe this water! It will drown you.

Once I accepted the fact that I could not control other people and nothing in this world is perfect, it freed me. Freed me from a weight that was so heavy it consumed my life. It freed me from expecting to live a perfect life that does not exist.

I lacked contentment. I was never satisfied. I wanted everything to be great. I had to understand that greatness does not equal perfection. There are many great things that are not perfect. You can have a great life, career, or relationship. You can have a great house, car, dog, or church you attend, a great spirit, personality, or smile. None of these are perfect. All have flaws and imperfections. It does not remove the greatness. Nothing will be perfect, **but** God. No matter how long I live, this will hold true.

I encourage you to find what you need to let go. For me it was trying to be perfect. It was wanting others to treat me how I treated them. It was not allowing for mistakes. It was allowing my creativity to determine my standards of life. It was not accepting life's setback. It was me wanting to be great instantly and not accepting the process. I had to let go of the fact that I was not where I wanted to be in life. I had to let go of my failures and disappointments. I had to even let go of people. Sweet Jesus! Talk about difficult.

What is it that you need to let go? Betrayal, abandonment, and abuse are some heavy hitters. You still must let the pain and hurt go. If someone you trusted betrayed you, let it go. If you were abandoned as a child and it is affecting your life, seek counseling so you can let that pain and hurt go. Holding on to past hurt, disappointment, being treated unfairly, losing out on a job opportunity, not being as successful as planned, unhealthy relationships, negative thoughts, and feelings of entitlement need to be released. The past cannot be changed; being hurt, crying, upset, and angry does not erase what happened. The best thing you can do is let it go. What is holding you back? Why have you allowed it to take control? What will you do about it? Will you finally let it go?

I had to learn that life goes on no matter what the hiccups are in life. It could be great, good, bad, or broken. Nothing can change what has already happened and getting worked up over it is a waste of time, energy, and emotion. The past cannot be changed. You cannot reverse it. That part is over. Take a deep breath, and let it go. Let it go!§

Charmion Sparrow

Do Not Worry

Perfecting and mastering the concept of not worrying is probably one of the most difficult things I had to do. First of all, as I stated, I was a perfectionist. I was consumed with keeping my life perfect. With little to no money, I needed to pay my bills on time, make sure my son had everything he needed for college, make sure my parents were ok, make sure I had enough money to travel back and forth from Orlando to Atlanta. I needed to find my next source of income to keep me going. I needed to network and try to search for my next acting gig. I needed to do everything under the sun that "normal" people do. This stressed me completely out. I could barely do any of it. All I did was think about what I could not do and how things were not working out. I could barely sleep because my mind could not rest thinking about my next move. I was in panic mode worrying about what I could make happen. All I really needed to do was not worry.

Worrying about my situation and circumstances did not make things happen any differently. The outcome was the same whether I worried or did not worry. Worrying did not pay the bills; it did not help with my son's college tuition, did not buy my plane tickets back and forth to see my parents, did not keep a roof over my head, did not put gas in my car or food on my table. Worrying did not book me that commercial or tv gig either. All worrying did was take up space in my mind and consumed it with disappointment, sadness, and thoughts of being a failure. All it did was prevent me from having a good night's rest, gain weight from stress eating, and isolate myself from friends and family.

Worrying is a thief. It will rob you of many things. Do not allow worry to take away your quality of life. It may be difficult at times. I never said it would be easy. Just make the effort and take the steps necessary to avoid the worry. Move forward and leave the worrying behind.

If the rent is due and there is no money in the bank it is hard not to worry. I get it, trust me. If you receive an eviction notice, no amount of worry will make it go away. Figure out what your next move will be and do not worry about it. Make a plan. Sitting around worrying will not stop the eviction.

Evictions usually require a 30-day notice. This means you have 30 days to figure it out. So, what is the plan? Make some calls and see who can help. Contact local organizations, churches, family, and friends. Find out if there are any resources available. Figure out where your belongings will go if nothing comes through in time. Call local shelters. YES! Stop being so prideful. Things happen, adjust and make the best of it. If you must live in your car, you would not be the first, and I promise you will not be the last. Start eating all the food from the freezer and refrigerator to avoid throwing food away. Set aside items that can be easily stored and eaten without refrigeration or heating. These are things that can be done in this particular situation. It is not the best circumstance, and it will

Drowning

not be like this always. The better prepared you are, the easier it will be to endure this difficult time.

The main thing that helped me not to worry was literally accepting the fact that worrying did not change anything. All it did was make things worse. Have you ever tried to do a task and came up with a solution that only made it worse? People use the phrase all the time, "Stop because you are only making things worse." If worrying only makes things worse, why do we continue to do it?

The perfectionist in me activated my worry. Because things in my life were not what I considered perfect or moving fast enough, I consistently worried. I had to accept people for who they were or circumstances below my standards. If it was not my way, I had to be ok with it. Even if it is clearly wrong, it was still ok.

Do not let worry set in and take over your mind. It is one of the worst mind fillers you can have. Instead, replace it with a plan. What are you worried about? What has it robbed you of? Is it worth it? What is your plan?

Smile and Choose Happiness

Another lesson I had to learn is that I control my own happiness. If I am not happy, I am the only one to blame. I am not suggesting that things do not happen in life that are disappointing, frustrating, mentally exhausting, or emotionally taxing. I am also not stating that you can avoid being down. Having feelings of sadness will hit you from time to time. Where there is happiness, sadness can be lurking around the corner. What I am conveying is that sadness is something you can control. The time you allow it to resonate in your life is under your command. If you choose to be sad for a second, minute, hour, or day, it is completely up to you. Think of it like this. Sadness is you feeling down or low. Take sadness as being equal to falling on the ground. Many things can happen that can make you fall on the ground. You could trip over a stomp. You could miss a step. You could trip on your shoestrings. You could be pushed down by someone that made you fall. You could have gotten tangled up in something. All these things can happen to make you fall. Once you are on the ground you must decide what to do next. Remember that being on the ground equals sadness. How long will you be sad? Do you get back up right away and dust yourself off? Do you sit there for a minute and try to figure out how you fell in the first place continuing in sadness? Do you stay on the ground because you are embarrassed that you fell? Do you stay on the ground because you feel like you are too weak and cannot get up? Do you stay there because you want someone to pick you up? Do you stay on the ground because no one noticed you, and you need the attention the fall would bring? Do you stay there because you want to be pitied? Do you stay on the ground because you feel safe and do not want the risk of falling again? Do you stay there because there are no expectations from you when you are on the ground? Do you stay on the ground because that's what you have been taught to do? Do you stay there because society says it is normal to fall in your circumstance? Do you stay on the ground because you do not know how to get up? Do you stay there because someone pushed you down? Do you stay on the ground because you cannot believe life happened? Do you stay there because it just simply hurts too much? Do you stay on the ground because you feel as though you are just too weak to get up? Do you stay there because no one has told you all you have to do is get up? I am telling you now that all you must do is get up. There are moments of sadness in everyone's life, and you still must get up. You cannot stay on the ground. Staying there only allows the water of life to rise up. Eventually it will cover your entire body. Now you are completely under water. - Water that you can't breathe! You must get up before you drown. Get up! Use everything you have. Just get up!

If the doctor diagnoses you with cancer, you will more than likely fall to the ground. This is terrible news. Sadness will appear. How long you allow it to stay is your choice. Will you stay on the ground for weeks and cry woe is me? Will you shake the dust off overnight and say I cannot change this, so let me be my best me? Will you fight it and make the best of your life? Will you seek out specialist and try to get the best treatment?

Let us look at the loss of a loved one. I do not know anyone personally that lost a loved one and was jumping up and down with joy. This is never easy. Whether the loved one lived a long life, had a sudden death, anticipated death, or tragic death, it is something that we all will deal with. This will indeed bring out the emotions of sadness. This is a natural feeling and common thing. No one expects for you to be happy at the onset of the loss. Being depressed about it will not bring them back or add to your life. What you must do is determine how long you will allow sadness to take up residence in your life. You can dwell on it. In the end it does not change anything. How long you decide to be sad about the situation is only going to keep you from being happy and living your best life.

Sometimes our falls are avoidable. This means some sadness can be avoided. Stop allowing the same sadness in your life. Keeping with the same analogy, stop falling the same way. If you fell because you tripped over your shoestrings, tie your shoes. If you fell because someone pushed you down, do not allow them to keep pushing you. If you fell because you did not see the rock in the road, pay attention to where you are going next time. Stop being sad because you fell. Get up! It is that simple.

Some falls are not that serious. We make them larger and more devastating than they must be. Was your fall minor or major? Did your fall just bruise your knee? Did it break your leg? Were you even hurt by it? Some people are sad for no reason. They fell over a rock they did not see coming. Sadness is on the ground. They are just sitting there being sad. They are not hurt by the fall. They are just on the ground and will not get up. I have literally asked someone before why they were so sad, and they told me they did not know. It blew me away.

Sadness is easy. It does not take any effort or work. If you want to be sad all you must do is stay on the ground. You do not have to move. No one expects anything from you when you are on the ground. Life is put on hold. You think it is safe because as long as you are on the ground you cannot fall again. This is a misconception because there are consequences with staying on the ground too long. You become more stiff and weaker from no movement. Now it is harder to get off the ground. Because it is harder you stay there even longer. You are convinced it is just easier to sit on the ground and wait until it is all better. Breaking News, you cannot get better on the ground. You must find the strength to get up before it leads into a lengthy cycle of sadness. Getting up is the beginning of your happiness.

Happiness takes work. Effort must be made in order for happiness to dwell in your life. It is not easy. It takes coordination and skill. You may have to dodge, jump over, push away or even change coarse to avoid sadness in order to maintain your happiness. You must learn how to get up off the ground when life knocks you down. It is a process, and it takes practice.

People get up differently, and no two people are alike. Some may use their hands more to get up, and others may use their legs more. Some may roll over to the side and put one leg up and stand. However, how you decide to stand is up to you. It takes effort. This skill can become easy the more you practice it. When you practice happiness, like practicing anything else, you become strong. The stronger you are the easier it is to get up from a fall. Exercise being happy. Do something every day that makes you smile. You are in control of your happiness. No one can make you happy.

Bottom line, sadness can only last if you allow it. Sadness is under your control. You must decide how long you stay on the ground. It is more of a choice and less of a feeling. If you are not happy with something, change it!

Train Your Mind

Have you ever met people that were just happy all the time? Every time you see them there is a smile on their face. Sometimes they even seem to cheer you up. It is because they practice happiness. It is a part of them. They think positive thoughts. They do not let the cares of the world get them down. It is not because unfortunate things do not occur in their lives. It is how they view them. How they let it affect them. They have trained their minds. They are in tip-top shape in maintaining positive thoughts which keep negativity at bay.

There are others that are not so optimistic. When the sun is not shining bright, they will turn a light overcast into a thunderstorm. It is those you hate to see coming because all they do is complain. They never have anything good to say. The energy they give off is exhausting, draining, and leaves you feeling fatigued. You frown before they open their mouth. Their mind has been trained to only see the bad. It is heavy and weighted down. Their brain is entirely out of shape. It is very weak when it comes to thinking happy thoughts. Instead of acknowledging that things could be a lot worse than they are they accept complete failure. Nothing in between. These are the ones you should avoid. It can be contagious if your mind is not strong in thinking happy thoughts.

Now, let us talk about your brain. Do you have a fatty brain? Is it lazy? Is it energized? Is it weak or strong? Are your positive thoughts, which are your lean and healthy muscles, stronger than your negative thoughts, which are the extra pounds of fat? What type of weights are you lifting? Is it happiness, positivity, and accomplishments? Or is it sadness, negativity, and failure? Are you running toward your goals or are you sitting on the couch feeling sorry for yourself? Are you bench pressing the bad karma away or letting the bar crush your chest? Are you punching negativity in the face or are you allowing the punching bag to swing back and knock you down? Are you squatting on depression or are your legs too weak?

You must put your mind through a mental bootcamp. You must train your mind like you train your body when exercising. You must burn away the fat, which are the negative thoughts around each circumstance. When negative things try to creep inside your mind you will be strong enough to fight it without question. When bad things occur, the effects will not be as detrimental when the mind is strong. A strong mind will allow you to see the light at the end of the tunnel.

Experts have stated that muscle burns fat. People who are muscular and lean tend to burn off more calories. They can eat a huge slice of cake and their body will just burn it off. While on the other hand the cake you ate is sticking to your hips and thighs. Is that fair? Absolutely! They put in the work to be able to eat that slice of cake preventing it from going straight to their hips and thighs. This mind transformation of thinking positive thoughts is similar. Do not allow the bad thoughts to stick to your mind and control your thoughts.

The weight of the world will only sit on your mind if you have not trained it and built up your brain muscle. You must push your mind to think positive thoughts. You must not only tell yourself things will get better, you must believe it. The stronger your mind is against negativity, the less you are weighted down with bad emotion and feelings of failure.

Sometimes things will happen in your life that will literally make you want to throw up as if you were overworked by a fitness trainer. If you quit because you feel like you are going to throw up, you will never get the results you want. It is the same when thinking positive thoughts. Even when things are falling apart and your initial thoughts are bad, you must think and meditate on the good in it. Keep thinking of what good can come out of it. This can sometimes seem impossible. You must find your light in the darkness. If you do not, you will not be able to see your way out. Just like you push your body through the pain when exercising, you must push your mind toward positive thoughts.

When people exercise and push their bodies to the point of pain and fatigue, they do it because their thoughts are positive. They are thinking this hurts now, despite that, I will have that lean and slim physique if I push through the pain. You must continue to push your mind to the next level for you to get results, even through the pain. Even after you have accomplished your goal of thinking positive, you must keep working on a consistent basis so it will remain.

People who work out routinely stay fit. They do not allow the bad stuff they occasionally eat to take over their bodies. They continue to work out so when they happen to occasionally eat something unhealthy, it does not affect them.

It is totally how you view things that matter the most. Two people can experience the same situation and view them very differently. Strong mental, positive thoughts will determine the work you need to acquire. How would you view this next situation? Are you weak or strong?

There was a storm that hit a small town. Many families had to seek shelter. Once the storm was over, they returned to find out all the houses were destroyed. One man complained the entire time about how he had lost so much. The other one was grateful his family was still alive and focused on the few items and valuables that could be salvaged. Clearly no one wants to lose their home and possession. Being down and out and thinking negative thoughts will not reverse the storm. It will not restore your lost items or your home. All it does is weigh you down. Keep you low. Make you feel heavy and out of breath. It is draining. It can lead to depression. Once you allow those bad thoughts, that are in the form of fat, to take over, you become fat minded. Do not do it. Trust me, it is as hard as trying to lose extra body fat.

I had to learn to think positive, and this was not always easy. When things happened that did not go my way, I focused on the good things. I could not pay all my bills, yet I could pay my energy bill. I could not go out to eat like before, although my refrigerator was full of food. I did not book the role on the tv show, instead I got an opportunity to network and meet with the casting directors. I did not get the job I applied for, at the same time, I had more applications out there, and I will get the job that's right for me. I had to continue to focus on positive things in my life. It kept me feeling light and energized to make it through the day. It allowed me to want to see better things that lie ahead. When you think things will only get better, you look forward to the days ahead. Do not allow your mind and the extra weight of this world weigh you down to the point that you do not care about what lies ahead. Do not get to the point where you cannot wait for the day to be over. When your life is to the point where the weight of the world leads to wishing each day were shorter and shorter, this is dangerous. Depression has taken over. You can't breathe water. You must burn those negative thoughts off before you drown.

Depression is like extra weight. Depending on how many pounds you must lose, the harder and longer it will take to get rid of it. Do not give up. So, you ate those cookies. Eat better tomorrow and keep it moving. Just do not give up, even when you have minor setbacks. This is the same when you are exercising your mind, and you slip up sometimes with bad thoughts. Do not allow it to take over. If today was so hard you just want to cry, cry, then do something that makes you happy. If you are overwhelmed and do not know where to start, make a list and start with one. Exercise good thoughts and train your mind to believe you will sometimes stumble. You may even fall; nevertheless, you will never fail.

Your mind is the strongest part of your body. The brain controls everything. How you think determines how you live. How you think determines every decision you make in life. If we can change how we think, depression has no control. Learn to be an optimist. Think positive!

Sing a Song

What in the world does singing have to do with anything? This question is on the mind of both, the singer and non-singer. Furthermore, if you are not a singer, you immediately rejected the thought. If you are a singer your thought is, "Why?" How can singing help me when I am drowning in life's obstacles? How can singing erase my pain, soothe my soul and get rid of my frustrations? How can it help me overcome my depression? I will tell you.

I have not studied music therapy; nevertheless, there is something very true about how it affects your emotional well-being. It is good for the soul. Singing will change the direction of your situation like nothing I have ever experienced. Singing can make an unpleasant situation tolerable. It can produce a refreshing atmosphere. It can exhaust a fiery situation. Singing can wash pain away. It is like a band aid with Neosporin. If you keep applying it daily, it will heal the wound as if it were never there. It is powerful!

I have not met anyone singing a happy song with full voice in a bad mood. It is impossible. If people could just sing a happy song, it would make them feel better.

Just start singing, "I'm happy, so happy, just happy." Sing it however you like, fast or slow, just do it with high energy and a gigantic smile on your face.

If you did it, your mood should have change. It is like magic! It is the secret antidote to a bad, frustrating, or sad situation.

The harder it is to sing a happy song the more likely you need to sing it. There are times when the very last thing you want to do is talk let alone sing. This is the moment you give it all you have. Do not let your thoughts or feelings get in the way of you singing. Sing yourself happy. Sing until you feel better.

Make a list of happy songs. The last thing you want to do is try to think of a song when you are stressed out or in the moment of need. These songs must be pre-selected. They should be categorized and used at the appropriate time. You should have a song for times when you are stressed out. A song when people are getting on your nerves. A song when you are feeling overwhelmed. A song when you want to express yourself in an unpleasant manner because someone has pissed you off. Your list can be long or short. Just have it ready.

You also need a pocket song. A pocket song is one you have at all times. Think of it as being in your back pocket. The one you always carry around with you. A short little song. A song covering multitude of situations and circumstances. It can be a chorus of a favorite song or one that is made up.

My pocket song is one I created with my son. It is a simple song, yet it covers a variety of situations. It is the song I use every day when little mishaps try to come and steal my joy. I sing it when someone has road rage, cuts me in line, tries to take advantage of me, when I become impatient, or someone gets on my nerves. It is also the song I sing when things are going right. It a song of gratefulness. It reminds me of who I am.

I remember a time when I was on the phone with a customer service agent trying to resolve an issue. She was not helpful at all. I just wanted to speak to a manager. She insisted the manager would only tell me the same thing. I did not care. I just wanted to speak to the manager. She continued to explain I would be on hold for an extended period of time if I waited. I just started singing my pocket song on the phone. She became confused. She could not understand why I was singing. This made me laugh, and it made her laugh as well. It changed my mood, and I became more patient. The issue was resolved without the manager. This may not be the case for you; yet, it worked for me.

My son would call me singing our pocket song. I would ask him, "Is it good or bad?" We would both laugh before he answers. Sometimes it would be good and other times a stressful situation. You cannot get millennials to do anything unless they see the benefit. He does it without thinking about it. There must be a benefit. It is hilarious when we are together, out in public, and one of us begins to sing. We can hardly contain ourselves because we know why we are singing. Someone or the current situation is frustrating us, and we just start singing. If he starts singing, I can barely contain myself. It is so hilarious! When I'm laughing at him, he immediately starts laughing back. The mood changes and we move on.

Just the topic of this section will increase the eyebrows of many readers. Most will think I am stretching the envelope. Do not be deceived. Do not toss this aside. It may be the one thing you need the most. Open your mind and change your thoughts. Make your list. Sing a song! It will bless you.

Get Active

One of the things you must do to just live a happier life and stay out of that unhappy place is to get out and be actively engaged with people. Hear me clearly, with people. Find something you like doing to have fun. Find people that like the same things, and do it with them. If it is shopping with your girlfriends, eating at new restaurants, playing games, going to the movies, reading books, cooking, fishing, playing sports, horseback riding, cycling, working out, doing cross word puzzles, gardening or even taking pictures, find others to do it with you. Whatever it is that you like doing, do it with other people. Engaging in activities with likeminded individuals give you some time to break your mind free from the everyday cares of the world. It also allows you to do something you enjoy doing and laugh. Laughter is good for the soul. Researchers have said that engaging with others or maintaining friendships increases your life span. It allows you to de-stress. This is particularly important in preventing yourself from slipping into depression or even trying to get yourself out of a depressed state. If you like fishing, it would be more fun with others that like to fish rather than doing it alone. You miss out on the celebration with someone when you have caught that big fish or the laughter behind you catching a ridiculously small one. If you like shopping, doing it with others is far more exciting than shopping alone. When shopping with your girlfriends, you are trying on items to see what they think, picking out items for them to try on, comparing items to see what looks good, receiving their opinion, and just enjoying the fellowship. This is important. If you are a foodie, go out and explore different restaurants with others. If cooking is your thing, invite me over from time to time to enjoy that wonderful meal. I will bring the wine. You can even teach others how to cook. If you like bowling, join a league. If you play sports, there are many different leagues for all ages and skill level. If you are a loner and like to be shut away from society, guess what, you are not the only one. Find more loners out there in the world and do whatever it is that you all enjoy. If you do not have friends or family to be active with, join a few meet up groups. There are literally meet up groups for everything and every activity. Bike riding, painting, acting, dancing, singing, gardening, sewing, and board gamers are a few popular ones.

You should not feel like it is a chore or obligation. If it does, you have either selected the wrong activity or you do not think you deserve it. You are focusing on the negatives and constantly complaining. I do not have any friends. I do not have the time. Everyone else is better than me. I do not have any money. This mindset is blocking you from becoming a better you.

If you do not have friends, this is the time to make some. There are groups you can join. Talk to people at your job. Connect with individuals at your local church or community center. To have friends one must show themselves friendly. I am not suggesting you be the creepy person that's on the hunt for friends. It is being open to engaging with others who like the same things you like or can connect on the same level. Maybe your child's friend from school has a parent that you can connect with. Join the PTA. Maybe there's someone that could use a workout partner at the gym you are attending. Friends are not hard to find. Do not let this be your reason.

If you have a busy schedule and do not have time for your own happiness, then you are saying you are not important. You may have to clean house before you make time for yourself. Do not let this linger. If you start out with only an hour a month for this activity, so be it. Maybe for you it can only be thirty minutes every other week. Whatever time you have, schedule it, and make it happen. Put it on your calendar and keep it. Do not allow anything to take up that space.

This also does not have to be a financial burden. You can find things that are free if finances are an issue. Research local event in your area. They have activities that are free going on all the time. The bottom line is to get active with people.

Have an activity to look forward to that does not have stress or is not motivated by obligations. Be open and dedicated to enjoying the things in life that make you happy and make lasting memories. This will allow you to de-stress. It will allow you to take a load off and to enjoy your life. All work and no play are what you should avoid. These are your mini mental vacations. It will allow you to rejuvenate.

The key is to be active at least twice a month. Find an activity that you can do with other people allowing you to be free and happy. The more you can find time to do this will have a tremendous effect on your happiness. Happiness and sadness do not mix. It is like oil and water. It is like being hungry or full. Both cannot exist at the same time. The more you feed yourself with happiness, the less times you will be hungry. Why starve yourself when you can eat?

The Why

There's not one person on this earth, if he or she had the opportunity, that would not change something from his or her past. If they had to do it all over again, they would do things differently. It is the familiar saying of hindsight is 2020. This is because life has taught us valuable lessons. If we had known then, what we know now, of course, the outcome may have been different. Roadblocks could have been avoided. A lot of time would not have been wasted. Plans and goals may have been achieved sooner rather than later. These thoughts of guilt and regret can weigh so heavy on the mind. All you can think about is how you did not get it right. Time is consumed with beating yourself up; you are questioning yourself repeatedly. Why me? How could I be so stupid? How could I let this happen to me? Why did I not choose the other route? Why did I not listen to my inhibition? Why am I not where I want to be in life? Why can I not find the right mate? Why do I hate my life? Why am I not successful? Why do people not like me? Why are doors being shut in my face? Why can I not catch a break? Why am I not happy? Why? Why? Why?

After all the questions begins justification. When you begin to justify your place of lowness, disappointment, or failure, you begin to accept where you are. You remove the option of positive change.

You believe that things are never going to get better because of what you have done or did not do. If you believe this, you are absolutely right. Things will never get better if you believe things will not change. If you believe your current situation or circumstance defines your path, it will. If you believe your past determines your future, it will. If you believe that your mistakes in life prevents you from moving forward, it will. If you believe you will never find the right mate, you will not. If you think you cannot catch a break, you will not. If you do not believe you can have a better life, it will not happen. Do not allow the "why" in your life keep you back and allow you to believe things will not get better or ever change.

We always have the question of, "Why?" It is often never answered. Do you know why you have not found the right mate? Do you know why doors are being shut in your face? Do you know why people do not like you? Do you know why you have not received that promotion? Do you know why you cannot pay your bills? Do you know why your siblings do not speak to you? Do you know why you have a bad relationship with your parent? Do you know why you are still in the same place you were 5 years ago? Do you know why you have not achieved your goals in life? Do you know why you are depressed? Have you answered these questions? Do you truly know the correct answer to your why? Have you guessed the answer, or did you research and seek to find the right one? Many of us cannot find the right mate because we are moving from mate to mate without knowing why we continue to enter bad relationships. Moving from relationship to relationship, or test to test, without truly knowing your why can lead to the same outcome. How can you find the right mate without truly knowing why your relationships have failed in the past? How can you advance if you do not pass the test? How can you pass the test without the right answers? Do you know the root cause or issue? Do you know why it continues to happen?

In math, there is a process and formula you must use to solve an equation. For example,
$$2+3\times4 =?$$
What is your answer? Some will say the answer is 14 and other may suggest it is 20. There is only one right answer. If you do not know the rules of math you may end of with the incorrect answer. If somehow your answers are not allowing you to pass the test, you may discover your answers may be incorrect. If you are trying to reach the next level or achieve your goals in life with the incorrect answers or solutions, it will not work. Will you search to find out what the answer is, or will you just go with what you think you know and continue to be stuck? Sometimes we get stuck on the simple things because we think it should be a no brainer. Taking the time out to make sure you get it right is important. Sometimes we must go back to the drawing board on things that we think we know to make sure we are certain.

To find out why people really do not like you, you must ask someone that does not like you. Why ask someone that likes you why others feel ill will towards you? Without going to the source, you may be operating with the wrong answers.

Do you know why doors are being closed in your face? Did you ask the door closer? Do you know why you are in the exact same place you were 5 years ago? Did you analyze your life?

If you keep taking the same test multiple times with the same wrong answers, what outcome can you expect? It does not matter if you change the pen color, use a pencil, write in pen, or use cursive writing, incorrect answers will not produce a passing grade. Without a passing grade, it is almost impossible to move to the next level. Take the test and discover your why.

There are five types of people when it comes to test taking. Depending on the situation you are facing will determine your type. Unfortunately, bouncing between the multiple types are not only common; it is also normal as well.

The first type are the *guessers*. They are the individuals who want things quick without putting in the effort to learn. They just keep trying different things until they get it right. They will take the test and apply the effort without doing the research. They would rather just keep trying over and over until they get it right. This amount of effort can become very exhausting. The effort is sometimes so great that fatigue sets in, followed by an unachieved goal. They are super busy doing everything they know to do to achieve their goal or pass the test and have not dug deep enough to find the true answer. They operate with self-taught knowledge, their own common sense, or outdated methods. They utilize these operations until they get it right. These are usually the highly educated and artistic individuals. They are the critical thinkers. The ones who usually figure things out with decent results. They are naturally talented. They obtained a lot of small accomplishments on their own. The issue with this is no one is always right. Many times there could be a better and more efficient way. Just because it is working does not mean it is right. Just because you were able to get where you are today on your own does not mean you can continue to grow with the same knowledge. Stop guessing. It is a waste of time and energy. Many times, it does not work. It may sometimes get you to the next level, although just like a test, guessing your way through it and not learning the information makes the next level much harder even if it is achieved. Beware, achieving the next level through guessing can also lead to a false sense of accomplishment.

Then you have the *avoiders*, the ones who think the test is too difficult. They do not put any time or effort in trying. They do not like confusion or confrontation. They avoid it at all costs. They allow themselves to be defeated without trying. They are lazy. They expect life to be easy breezy. They want things to get better on their own. They want to reap the reward without taking the test at all. They want to know why they do not have a relationship with their family and avoid asking them why. They want to know why their health is failing and avoid going to the doctor. They want to know why their spouse is angry and not speaking to them, and they never ask. These are people that are quick to ask the questions but ok with leaving them unanswered. THEY SETTLE.

Then we have the *amateurs*. The unskilled and inexperienced individual that just goes through life doing things the same way without growth or change. They think they know all the right answers. They are extremely comfortable doing it the old way. They have the basic skills and need to enhance them to progress to the next level. They want things to get better doing it the incorrect or inefficient way. They are stuck on what worked in the past that does not work today. They struggle to get to the next level. They are closed minded when it comes to change and do not want to be trained. They would rather use a flathead screwdriver with a phillip screw. They would rather use plain flour instead of self-rising flour. They would rather use a typewriter instead of a computer. They would rather write a check then use a debit card. They would rather wait in a long line at the bank to make a deposit instead of using the ATM. They would rather do it the only way they have been taught than to learn a new way or approach. These are the ones that are stuck and never progress.

Believe it or not there are some that have the answers and do not apply it. They have taken the time to research what needs to be done and do not want to exert the effort in achieving it. Thinking about it is exhausting to them. They feel like it is too much to achieve. They do not feel like they deserve it. They feel like they are not good enough. They do not apply it because it is not what feels good. It is not what they expected. It is not easy. They do not want to accept it. They do not believe they can do it, so they also settle.

This type is similar to the avoiders. They are called the *slackers*.

Finally, we have the *progressors*, the ones who take the time to study, learn and pass the test. These are the ones that get it done. They have had ups and downs, roadblocks, and setbacks, and they keep on going. They study the situation, goal, problem, and learn what it takes to produce a favorable outcome. Growth happens and goals are eventually achieved. Sometimes it takes mentors, life coaches, focus groups and counseling to be a progressor. It also takes great discipline and determination. What type of test taker are you?

I was drowning. You can't breathe water. Nothing seemed to be working, and I did not know why. Initially I did not take a step back to see why things were the way they were. I just questioned it. I got stuck in the why. I got stuck in the fact that I was trying to do better. I was working hard. I was a good person. I was educated and smart. I was determined to be great and make things happen. I was strong. I was not going to give up or be defeated. Even with that mindset, I was still drowning. I was slipping away and wasting a lot of time and energy doing things with the wrong answers. I was always saying, "Why Lord?" and "Why me?". I had to figure out why the water in my life was trying to drown me. I had gone out to sea too far and I was not prepared for the heavy waves. I was a guesser and an amateur at the same time. I was able to achieve certain things on my own, with my own knowledge and skills. I am creative, artistic, and analytical. I was able to make it far out in the ocean and did not have all the right equipment when I got there. When the storm came, I was not prepared and did not have all the skills I needed once it was time to weather the storm.

When I realized I was drowning, I had to take a step back and determine how to become the progressor. I needed the answers to my "Why's" in life and when I got them, things changed. I was able to understand why I was in my current situation and things were stationary in my life. I was able to grasp why I was not growing and accomplishing the things that I wanted or desired in life.

One of the reasons was my relationship. It was stressful. I entered a relationship trying to fill a void in my life. This is one of the main issue relationships go sour and can't be restored when the storms of life happen. Rather than choosing a person out of compatibility, it is out of feelings and emotions. They temporarily cover up what is truly going on in your life and allow you to forget what you are currently dealing with. This is only a temporary fix and often never works out. I did not realize this at the time. I thought I was in a good place because I was not carrying baggage from a previous relationship. I worked on trying to make things better within the relationship because I believed no relationship was perfect.

My relationship was different. We were not compatible, and it was not his fault the relationship did not work. I could point blame. When I take the strong assessment, it was truly all on me. The more I was stressed out the more I stressed him out. When he became unhappy, like many men, he tapped out. I expected him to relieve my stress or at least not add to it. He could not fix what he did not break.

We were also not emotionally or spiritually connected. This would have definitely helped. It just was not the person he was. We also spoke different languages. It was far different then apples and oranges, it was more like apples and onions. We were not even in the same category. I was on the fruit aisle, and he was on the vegetable aisle. Rarely we both ended up with a tomato, which some would argue if it were really a vegetable or fruit.

So, what did we have? A great time going out, I mean the absolute best time. He was like an ice cube on a hot summer day. Very refreshing, but ice always melts in the heat. This is what my relationship was created on. Fun times and laughter. That's all we had.

I entered the relationship before I was genuinely happy and at peace with myself, which was a mistake. The compatibility was not there, and because I needed a distraction, it was better than nothing. No matter what I did, nothing changed that made it better.

I grew and learned a lot within the relationship. It made me a better person. It is just that the relationship itself was not something I needed at the time. It was not healthy, and neither was I. You must determine if the relationship you are in was created on an ice cube cooling you down, or if it is just a storm cloud that must be weathered. No relationship will be without tension at times because no two people are alike. Just make sure you are putting the work, time, and energy into something that will grow and change. Do not spend time trying to put a square into a circle. It will never work, no matter how hard you try.

Another one of my "why's" was not getting cast or booked for roles when I moved to Atlanta. I just accepted that I was not good enough. I did not tackle it by going to a different agent or enrolling in classes to increase my skill set. I gave up. This was a big one because it was my goal in life. Acting was what I aspired to do. It was my main purpose for moving to Atlanta. I had sacrificed my life by putting my dream on hold for so long to give my son a more stable life. My dream did not work as I planned, so I gave up. Even though I gave up trying I did not give it up in my heart. I still wanted to accomplish it. Because there was no release, it weighed me down. The weight came from not being able to move on. Sometimes there will be dreams and goals in life that we may not be able to achieve. It is not the lack of achievement that weighs us down. It is the fact that we cannot let go and move on. We cannot accept defeat. Everyone loses sometimes. We cannot win at everything because everything is not for us. It is that simple.

One more "why", I was very unhappy about the way I looked. I had gained a lot of weight. I was the largest I had ever been. I was consistent with my diet and exercise. My scale was consistent as well by not decreasing my pounds of fat. I tried every diet. Nothing seemed to work. I was not dropping a pound. When I had gained weight in the past, I committed to a diet and exercise regimen and lost the weight. This time it was different. The difference that I discovered was that my hormones were out of whack. No matter what I did, the weight was not coming off until I was able to control them. There was no way to do this with my level of stress.

Life is full of test. Without passing them you will never get to the next level. Some answers are easier than others. Others take research and effort. If you have questions that have you in a low place or preventing growth, seek to find answers. Be the progressor. Learn and grow. It is the best way.

Find Your Peace

Peace is defined as freedom from disturbance; tranquility, or a state or period in which there is no war. Some of us are disturbed by how we look or how we view ourselves. We are disturbed by the lack of friends we have. We are disturbed by the lack of functionality in our lives. We are disturbed with obtaining financial freedom. We are disturbed by what someone has said or how someone is treating us. We are disturbed by other's lack of knowledge; disturbed by other's actions; things are not being done how we would like them; things are not happening as fast as we think they should. There is no peace. Everything is in an uproar.

We are at war on the job or at war with our children or spouse. We are at war with family members and friends. There are never moments of tranquility. The mind is constantly consumed with negativity from all the disturbances. These disturbances and wars are peace blockers. They block happiness, joy, comfort, smiles, energy, and rest. They also block growth and productivity.

When thinking about peace blockers, many can draw a quick conclusion to the ones that are present. The more common ones are dealing with a bad relationship, worrying about our health, thinking about the future and what it will or will not bring, controlling others and just wanting more in life (not being satisfied). There are several things that may not be considered as peace blockers because of its nature. Things like dealing with a rude and disrespectful boss, caring for elderly parents, raising children, unaccomplished goals, having too many responsibilities in life, or having an unforgiving heart. These things can block your peace as well.

My list of peace blockers was long. Once acknowledged, I was aware of what was going on and how I allowed things to block my peace. Protecting my peace was based on choices I needed to make based on each situation. At some point I had to realize what was more important. Was it my peace or the cares of this world and satisfying other people? I had to determine that it was my peace that would take precedence over the cares of this world and worrying about what others did or thought. It was my peace I needed to protect. I was the one in charge of making that happen.

One way to protect your peace is to create boundaries. Boundaries are important for everyone. If you have no boundaries in place, situations and individuals can easily disturb or rob you of your peace. Once boundaries are established, they should become your way of life.

When setting boundaries, they should be clear and precise. They should also be realistic and not situational. They should be centered around what makes you unpeaceful. When setting boundaries, you must only consider yourself. What can you tolerate? This should not be based on what other's feel you should be able to handle.

Determine your maximum tolerance level before your peace is disturbed and do not allow it to reach that level. Do not even allow it to come close. Why allow something or someone to reach your maximum level before you cut it off or back away from it?

I would often say to someone, "You have one more time to get on my last nerve." I had to protect my peace by not allowing it to get to that level. When thinking about this I could not understand why I even entertained them to the point where it reached my maximum tolerance level. They were not worth it. Oh, what a relief it was to just cut that off. I was taken back at how simple it was to avoid this peace blocker when boundaries were set. I was also disappointed in myself for allowing something so simple to disrupt my peace for so long. We live and learn.

I had to set a boundary over my finances. Although I was accustomed to certain things and a certain lifestyle, I was no longer in that state. I had to cut back. I could not continue spending the same way because I was not making the same money. My boundaries where: only eating out twice a month; not overspending in the grocery store; cutting back my cable package; doing my own hair, and limiting my extracurricular activities. After doing this I was able to manage my finances on a month-to-month basis, although my income was drastically lower. This clearly allowed a certain level of peace. It also taught me two things. One, I was spending too much money on things I did not need. The other one is that my life was not much different living without certain things that I thought I needed.

I also set boundaries on my expectations of others. I could no longer allow someone to get on my last nerve because of what I expected them to comprehend, accomplish, or communicate.

One of the things I had to do was to let people be stupid, ignorant, or misinformed. And sure, this is my opinion and fair to say because that's how I feel. Now at the same time, it does not mean they are stupid, ignorant, or misinformed; it is just how I viewed them. I had set a boundary in my mind that everyone will not get it. No matter how much you are willing to try to explain, compromise, sacrifice or extend grace, some will never cross over. Some will never make it to the next level. They will never graduate or meet their greatest potential. Some will stay stuck, and you will have to be ok with that. Their success or unsuccess should not be tied to your peace. If you are ever at a place that someone's growth or the lack there of is tied to your quality of life, you may need to reconsider your life, their purpose in your life, and your unrealistic expectation of others.

Another thing I had to do to protect my peace was to let some things be. I had to release control. I had to determine what I was going to take responsibility over, what I needed to control in my life. The less you control, the less you worry about. The less you worry about, the less stress you have. This leads to more peace. The lack of peace comes from having no control. It stems from the uncertainties in life, which again, we cannot control.

We are uncertain how things will work out. We are uncertain of what the future will bring. We are not secure financially. We are not secure in our relationships, job, or future. We have no control over how people treat us. No control over mishaps in life. No control over worldly disasters. So, what do you do? Stop trying to control the uncontrollable things in life. It is that simple. Set boundaries.

There is one final thing regarding your peace that should be done. I've listed it last, however, it was the major thing that helped me find, protect, and keep my peace. It is what I stand on and live by today. It is what keeps me strong, hopeful, and sane.

If you could literally just list all your peace blockers and hand it over, could you let it go? Would you put your trust in the process? Would you give it your all? If there was something that could handle everything that came your way no matter good or bad, would you jump on board?

I have great news. There is an ultimate peace provider. His name is Jesus! He will provide you a peace that exceeds all understanding. He will give you joy in the midst of a sad situation. He will give you rest when everything around you is falling apart. He will provide all your needs. The best part is that He will never fail you. All you must do is believe that He can, and He will. When you have peace in Jesus, no one can take that away, only you. If it does go away, it is because you have decided to give it back.

So, what must you do in order for Jesus to provide peace in your life? You must study the word of God. Find out what peace in God truly means. I could easily tell you, except I would only cover what is personalized for me. Because the peace blockers in life are different, what works for me will not work for you. Even if it is the same type of peace blocker. This is where the ball is often dropped. Picture this, two people are on the side of the road. Both have run out of gas. A gentleman stopped and offered to bring each of them back some gas to make it to the nearest gas station. As he drove off and quickly returned with one 5-gallon container of gas. He thought this would surely be enough to get them started and make it to the nearest gas station. Although this was indeed enough gas for both vehicle, one of them only used premium gas. Regular gas would not work for one of the vehicles. Although the issue was the same, them both needing gas, the solution to the problem was not. Some of us need a little more than others even when the situation or circumstance is the same. Both individuals needed gas even though the type of gas needed was different to make it to the next gas station.

Many times, we ask others for their advice far more often than we should. We want to solve our problems by what others have done. We try to resolve them by what seems to be the common fix. These can many times be helpful except when it comes to your peace; what works for others may not work for you. Sometimes it is better to research and get the correct information on your own. It is ok to seek guidance, however, not many people know your level of ignorance. They try to help you assuming you know more than you do. This can lead to failure. For example, Charlotte's friend, Anita calls and has a dilemma about cooking for a large group of people. It is explained that their cooking skills are extremely basic and catering food due to affordability is out of the question. Charlotte suggests to cook chicken. It is something everyone usually eats, and it can be very cost effective. Her cooking instructions are to season the chicken and cook it for about 25 to 30 minutes at 400 degrees. Charlotte suggests to complete the meal with a few simple sides. She also recommends to add a good salad option to cover any vegetarians. Seems pretty simple but there were issues that unfolded during this task.

First, the chicken was being cooked on a grill. Anita was trying to figure out the entire time how to get the grill at 400 degrees. Next, she had purchased drumsticks and wings. If you cook wings on the grill for 45 minutes, well, they are overcooked to say the least. Simple sides to me are things like rice, string beans, frozen veggies, or even mashed potatoes. Anita was in the store looking for something that was titled, "simple sides". Understanding the level to where the explanation needed to start prevented a successful outcome. Because it failed, Anita believed it would never work for her. This was hardly the case. Although Anita did state that her cooking skills where basic, that message did not come across as her not being familiar in the kitchen or with cooking terminology like "simple side". Often, we cannot even communicate where we need to start our learning.

This is the main reason it is important to get the information yourself. When you do this, it is valued, trusted, and believed without question. There is a difference between believing that God is a healer and knowing that God is a healer. There is a difference between someone saying that God is a provider and knowing personally that God is your provider. Likewise, when you get the word for yourself, and find out what God has to say about His peace, and believe it for yourself, your life will change forever.

I can teach you what I know; yet, I can only get you to understand something in the way I understand it. Many of us are going day to day without peace because we are relying on what other say about God's peace. Some think it does not work. It is because they have missed something that's tailored to them. This is because this world is made up of individuals who would rather pay for information instead of doing the research themselves. The problem is you may miss something that's key for you. It is the one little missing step or ingredient that prevents peace from happening. Only you know your specific detailed area of need. Only you know your weakness to the core. You may not even be able to communicate it properly to others; so how can you expect them to explain it to you completely? Everyone speaks different languages. Jesus understands them all.

We are unique in what drives, motivates and affects us. Because of this, you have to get your peace directly from the source that provides it. He is the only one who knows exactly what you need. He is the one that can restore your peace.

When I learned of God's peace, I learned that peace is not defined by the circumstance. Anyone, even you, can have peace in the midst of a terrible situation. The only way to totally understand that is through Jesus. Jesus is all you need. He will give you your peace back. When you have the peace that He provides, it will last. Protect your peace by setting boundaries, releasing control, and turning it over to God.

Conclusion

You can't breathe water! So, a decision had to be made. My decision was cut and dried. I was standing in the water, which meant I had the control to walk out on dry land. My feet were touching the ground. All I had to do was make a choice to allow the water to drown me or get out before it happened. I was standing straight up. I did not need any special skills. I did not have to know how to swim, float or tread the water. I did not need to do anything except make a decision to walk out of the water. All I had to do was decide that I did not want the things surrounding me to take over my life. I had to choose whether I would be defeated. I had to choose what was more important. Was paying my bills, having friends, reaching my goals in life, losing weight and the cares of this world more important than life itself? Was it worth losing my life over or being extremely depressed? No, absolutely not.

Depression is something that many will experience. Whether we recognize it as depression or not does not remove its existence. Just because it exists does not mean it has to remain.

If you walk away from reading this book and really believe that depression is a choice, you will never be depressed again. Will bad things happen in your life, absolutely? It is how we view or think about the situation that will determine how we respond. It takes work, and it does not happen overnight. The steps that prevented my mind from slipping into a depressed state will help you on your journey of thinking better. These steps helped me from feeling weighted down.

On your journey to stay above water, you must learn that you are most important. Learn who you are and figure out your purpose in life. Once you have done that, the road traveled is easy.

Practice letting things go to prevent stress in your life. Be active with people and create memories and joyous time to relieve some stressors in your life. Train your mind to think positive thoughts and to aim for an abundant life. Move to the destination that is beneficial, whether it be a physical place or an emotional place. Discover your purpose in life and live it. Find your peace and embrace it. Smile and choose happiness because you deserve it.

Let depression die. Bury it. Break up with it. Divorce it. Put it in the trash. Toss it in the lake. Kick it to the curb. Hang up on it. Do whatever you need to do to get rid of it. When you do, do not let it come back. No second chances. Let it go!

The task ahead is not easy; at the same time, it is not hard either. The hardest part is believing that you can overcome. Things will get better. No matter how low or difficult things may seem, the sun will come out tomorrow. When is your tomorrow? I do not know. Live your best life today until it does. Clean house, let stuff go, smile, choose happiness, train your mind, get active, discover your why and find your peace. Depression is a choice. Choose happiness.

You can't breathe water. You can't breathe water! You can't breathe water!! Decide, live or die! I decided to live, and I hope you do too. Depression is a choice. Choose happiness. You deserve it!

The End

ABOUT THE AUTHOR

A graduate of Florida A&M University, with a degree in Business Economics, proud mother of one son, fraternal twin, native of Orlando, FL., with a phobia of Corporate America, Charmion Sparrow is a force to be reckoned with. She has created, explored, and experienced many things throughout her life which has molded her into the woman she is today.

Her entrepreneurship extends through several platforms:

- Creator of a playing card game - www.OmariGames.com
- Songwriter – It's Your Birthday, Be Me, He Paid It All
- Sitcom writer – Gals, Miserably Single, Uncomplicated
- T-Shirt Company – www.TheDenomaShop.com
- Wine Label Designer
- Game Show Creator
- Actress

Always the busy bee, she found herself always searching for the next best thing. She was never fulfilled.

She could solve everyone's problems but her own. When the world started crashing down on her, she did what most would do who are strong in nature. She kept going. She kept pushing. She kept hoping. When that didn't work, she began to lose her way and depression set in. She speaks from the heart when she writes this book. Her desire is to help the individual that everyone thinks is strong and always on top. She is one who is always helping others, but never asks or expects help in return. The one who is so busy caring for others, when it is time for self-care, her well is dry. If the contents of this book reflect you, the read will be beneficial and therapeutic. Enjoy!

For Bookings:

- Happiness Is A Choice Workshops
- Book Writing Workshops
- Speaking Engagements
- Zoom Lessons
- 1 on 1 Chats
- Seminars
- Retreats

Go To:

www.DenomaPublishing.com

Or
Email:
BookCharmion@gmail.com

Bulk orders and workbooks are available.

Made in the USA
Columbia, SC
19 June 2024